SECRETS
OF THE
ANIMAL WORLD

SALMON
Tireless Travelers

by Andreu Llamas
Illustrated by Gabriel Casadevall and Ali Garousi

Gareth Stevens Publishing
MILWAUKEE

For a free color catalog describing Gareth Stevens' list of high-quality books and multimedia programs, call 1-800-542-2595 (USA) or 1-800-461-9120 (Canada). Gareth Stevens Publishing's Fax: (414) 225-0377. See our catalog, too, on the World Wide Web: http://gsinc.com

The editor would like to extend special thanks to Jan W. Rafert, Curator of Primates and Small Animals, Milwaukee County Zoo, Milwaukee, Wisconsin, for his kind and professional help with the information in this book.

Library of Congress Cataloging-in-Publication Data

Llamas, Andreu.
    [Salmón. English]
    Salmon: tireless travelers / by Andreu Llamas; illustrated by Gabriel Casadevall and Ali Garousi.
        p.   cm. – (Secrets of the animal world)
    Includes bibliographical references (p. 31) and index.
    Summary: Describes the physical characteristics, habitat, behavior, migration, ancestors, and predators of these efficient torpedo-shaped fish.
    ISBN 0-8368-1586-6 (lib. bdg.)
    1. Salmon–Juvenile literature. [1. Salmon.] I. Casadevall, Gabriel. II. Garousi, Ali. III. Title. IV. Series.
QL638.S2L5813   1996
597'.55–dc20   96-8199

This North American edition first published in 1996 by
Gareth Stevens Publishing
1555 North RiverCenter Drive, Suite 201
Milwaukee, Wisconsin 53212 USA

This U.S. edition © 1996 by Gareth Stevens, Inc. Created with original © 1993 Ediciones Este, S.A., Barcelona, Spain. Additional end matter © 1996 by Gareth Stevens, Inc.

Series editor: Patricia Lantier-Sampon
Editorial assistants: Diane Laska, Rita Reitci

Printed in the United States of America

1 2 3 4 5 6 7 8 9 99 98 97 96

CONTENTS

THE SALMON'S WORLD

Salmon habitat

Salmon are silver-colored fish with pointed heads that can measure 5 feet (1.5 meters) in length and weigh over 80 pounds (36 kilograms). They can live both in fresh water and sea water. Salmon belong to a family of animals called Salmonidae, which includes certain fish in the Northern Hemisphere. These animals live in cold waters, such as those of mountain rivers and lakes.

Salmon live in the clear, cold waters of the Northern Hemisphere.

Great travelers

Salmon are great travelers that take part in migrations over 1,250 miles (2,000 kilometers) long. After living in the sea for several years, they reach sexual maturity. Then they return to rivers, swimming upstream to the place where they were born. A salmon in the sea has white meat. A river-dwelling salmon has red meat.

The image of tireless salmon moving upstream has become famous all over the world.

Types of salmon

The Salmonidae family is a group of fish with sturdy bodies. They are all good swimmers. Their appearance changes according to age, sex, and sexual maturity. The most common salmon species fall into four groups, or genera. The *Salmo* genus includes salmon and sea trout. Both species can reach 5 feet (1.5 m) in length and weigh over 78 pounds (35 kg).

The *Salvelinus* genus includes fish that live in cold mountain waters. They travel upstream in autumn to lay eggs in winter, and they return in June. They can measure 32 inches (80 cm) and weigh up to 22 pounds (10 kg).

The *Oncorhynchus* genus includes fish over 1.5 feet (.5 m) in length that weigh up to 6.5 pounds (3 kg). These fish are a greenish brown color, with silver sides and belly.

The *Coregonus* genus includes fish up to 20 inches (50 cm) long. These fish are light-colored and spotted.

Coregonus
(whitefish)

Oncorhynchus
(Pacific salmon)

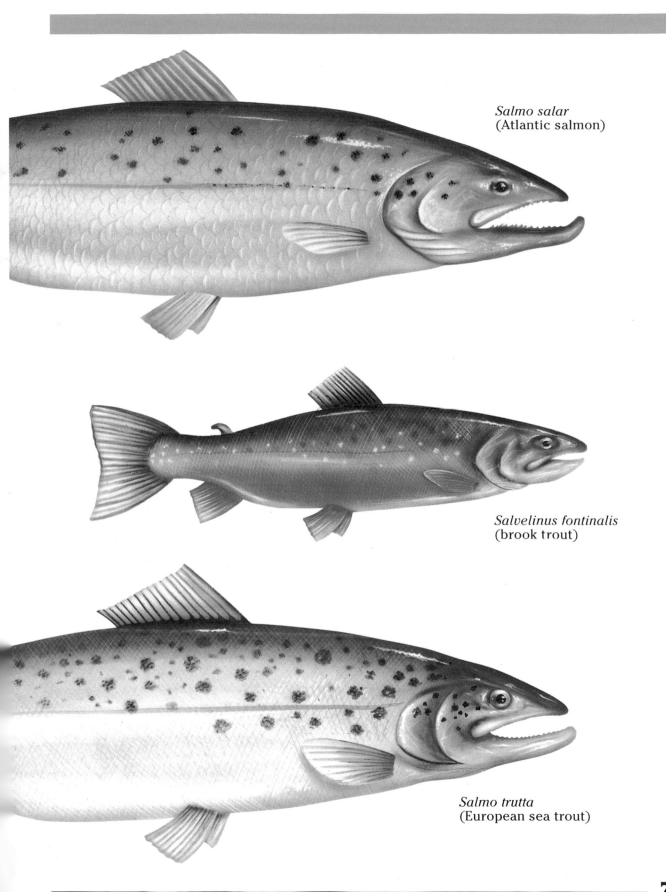

Salmo salar
(Atlantic salmon)

Salvelinus fontinalis
(brook trout)

Salmo trutta
(European sea trout)

INSIDE THE SALMON

The salmon's fusiform (torpedo-shaped) body and pointed snout allow it to glide smoothly through the water. Its fins move the fish forward and also direct and stabilize its movements. The salmon can breathe under water with its gills. The gills obtain the necessary oxygen for the salmon from the water.

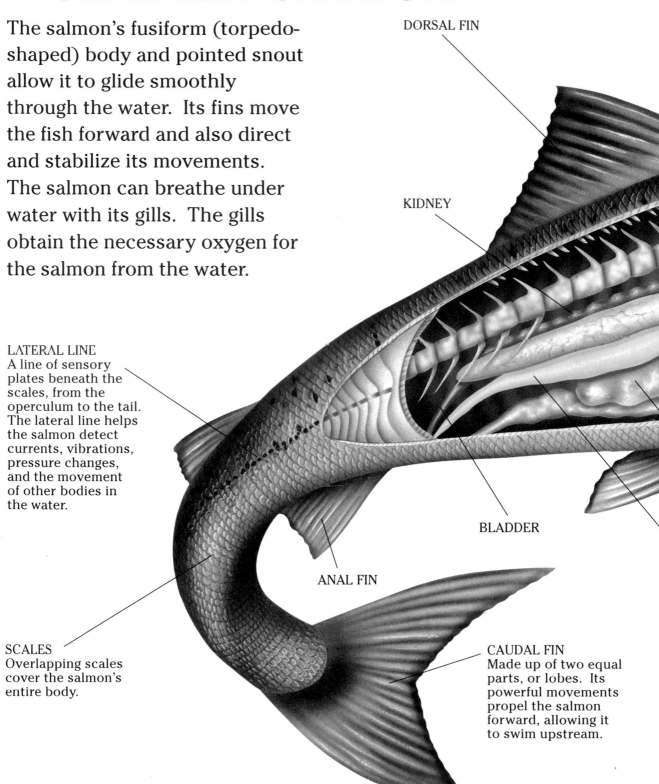

DORSAL FIN

KIDNEY

LATERAL LINE
A line of sensory plates beneath the scales, from the operculum to the tail. The lateral line helps the salmon detect currents, vibrations, pressure changes, and the movement of other bodies in the water.

BLADDER

ANAL FIN

SCALES
Overlapping scales cover the salmon's entire body.

CAUDAL FIN
Made up of two equal parts, or lobes. Its powerful movements propel the salmon forward, allowing it to swim upstream.

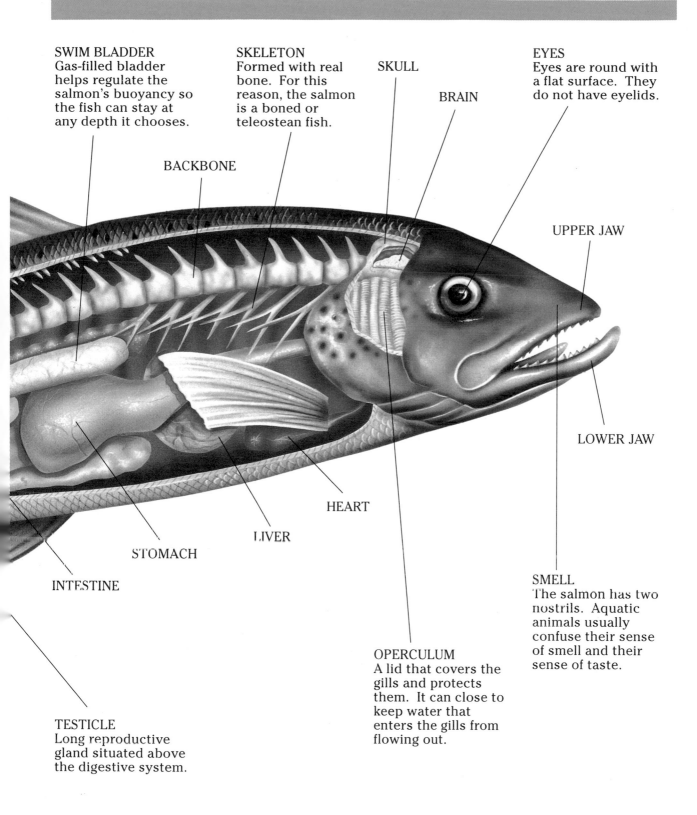

SWIM BLADDER
Gas-filled bladder helps regulate the salmon's buoyancy so the fish can stay at any depth it chooses.

SKELETON
Formed with real bone. For this reason, the salmon is a boned or teleostean fish.

SKULL

BRAIN

EYES
Eyes are round with a flat surface. They do not have eyelids.

BACKBONE

UPPER JAW

LOWER JAW

HEART

LIVER

STOMACH

INTESTINE

SMELL
The salmon has two nostrils. Aquatic animals usually confuse their sense of smell and their sense of taste.

TESTICLE
Long reproductive gland situated above the digestive system.

OPERCULUM
A lid that covers the gills and protects them. It can close to keep water that enters the gills from flowing out.

RIVER TO SEA TO RIVER

Young salmon hatch from their .3-inch (7-millimeter) eggs and soon learn to swim. For a few weeks, the young fish, called "fry," survive by eating insects and small aquatic animals. The fry spend between one and five years in fresh water. Then they follow an instinct to migrate to the sea. In each large group of

Newborn salmon live off their own food reserves for the first few days.

salmon, about 15 percent of the small fry die. If they manage to reach the sea, many are devoured by larger fish. From the thousands of eggs laid, only a small number of salmon reach adulthood. They complete their growth in the sea until they become adults — after one to six years. When the salmon are ready to reproduce, a strong migratory instinct urges them to return to their freshwater birthplace to reproduce.

After a period of one to five years, the young salmon start to move toward the sea.

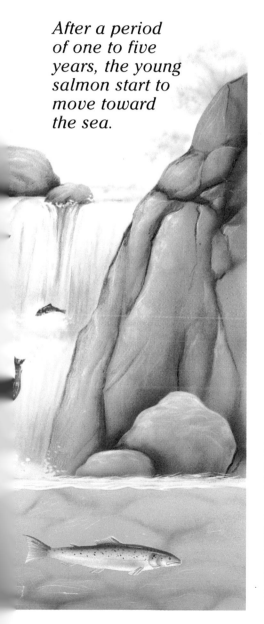

Young salmon complete their growth in the sea.

Returning to reproduce

Salmon travel great distances to reproduce. Migration is usually 125 to 185 miles (200 to 300 km) to their birthplace, but some travel more than 1,250 miles (2,000 km). Before the adult fish begins the migration from the sea to its birthplace, it stores large quantities of fat in its body. The fat is needed to provide energy for overcoming all the obstacles it might meet in its journey. The salmon does not eat while in fresh water. By the time reproduction is over, the fish has lost 40 percent of its weight, and most of the

Salmon always manage to find their birthplace.

Salmon can jump over 6.5 feet (2 m) high.

returning salmon die of physical exhaustion. Only 5 percent of the adult fish that make the voyage from the sea manage to survive. After a resting period of one to two years, these survivors return to the sea.

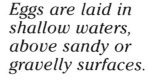

Eggs are laid in shallow waters, above sandy or gravelly surfaces.

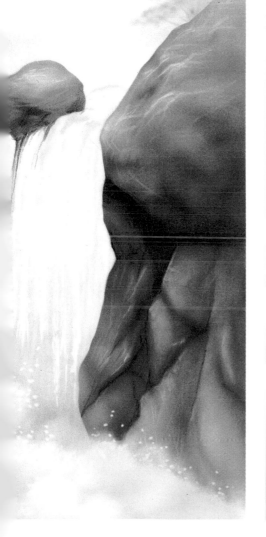

FINDING THE WAY HOME

How salmon swim

To reach their spawning ground, salmon have to swim upstream. They must struggle against swift currents, waterfalls, and hydro-electric dams.

Salmon have an impressive ability to jump. They can jump up to 13 feet (4 m) forward and 6.5 feet (2 m) high. To do this, they spring out of the water at 14 miles (23 km) per hour. The salmon's greatest speed over long distances is usually about 8 miles (13 km) per hour. In fresh water, the highest speed of small fish is about ten times their length per second, but this

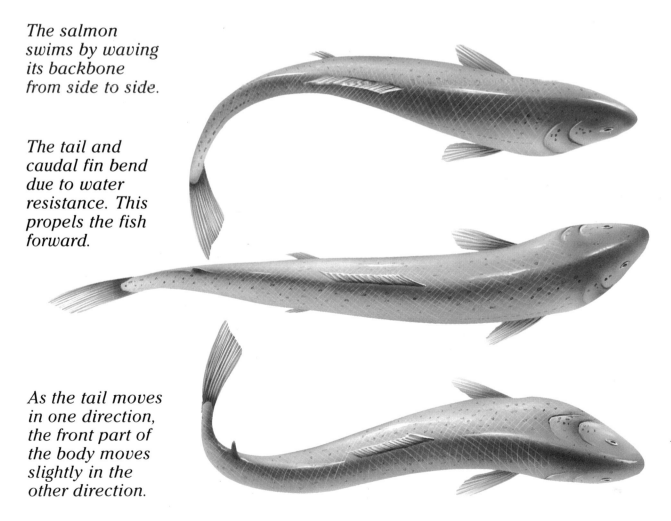

The salmon swims by waving its backbone from side to side.

The tail and caudal fin bend due to water resistance. This propels the fish forward.

As the tail moves in one direction, the front part of the body moves slightly in the other direction.

14

speed can only be kept up for a short time. The bigger the fish, the faster it can move.

Salmon can easily overcome small obstacles in the water with their amazing jumps. But when faced with the rushing waters of high waterfalls, they use another strategy. With giant leaps, the salmon move through the river's fast surface waters to reach an area where the speed of the current can be overcome with less difficulty. In this way, the salmon actually climb waterfalls by "swimming" upward.

With the help of its powerful tail, a salmon can overcome the resistance of strong currents and waterfalls.

that the salmon finds its way by smelling?

A salmon can find its birth-place with highly developed senses that allow it to recognize the temperature, smell, and chemical makeup of the water it was born in. Salmon find their way by "smelling" their route home. Every river has its own special smell. After birth, the salmon lives for a time in the stream. Years later, it remembers the smells and follows the trail home.

Mating dance

Female salmon prepare nests when they reach the spawning grounds. The nests measure 3 feet (1 m) in length and 2 to 4 inches (5 to 10 cm) in depth. They are always located parallel to the flow of the water current.

When the nest is ready, a "mating dance" between the salmon couple begins. The male swims around the female for a few minutes, biting her gills and belly. The female swims around, followed by the male. With its dorsal fin, the male touches the area where the eggs are to come out. After a while, the female drops a large number of eggs in the nest for the male to fertilize.

Salmon circle one another as they prepare to mate.

The female lays eggs in the nest. The male then fertilizes the eggs.

SALMON ANCESTORS

Primitive fish

Over 500 million years ago, the agnaths, or "fish without jaws," were the first vertebrates to evolve. Because these animals had no jaws, they were unable to catch and hold prey to feed themselves, so most of them were very small — only about 4 inches (10 cm) in length. They fed by sucking up plankton or microscopic particles from the seabed that could provide them with nourishment. Agnaths flourished for more than 135 million years in the seas, lakes, and rivers of the Northern Hemisphere.

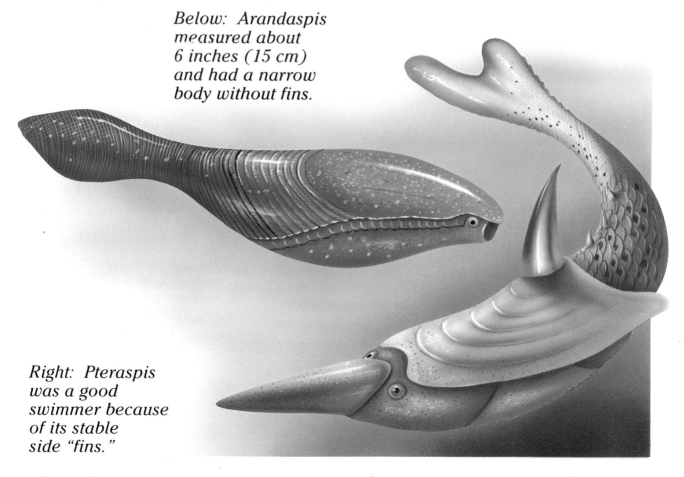

Below: Arandaspis measured about 6 inches (15 cm) and had a narrow body without fins.

Right: Pteraspis was a good swimmer because of its stable side "fins."

Armor-plated fish

About 400 million years ago, a group of jawed fish called placoderms appeared. The head and the front of these fish were covered in protective plates; the term *placoderm* means "plated skin." Most placoderms lived on the sea floor because of the heavy armor plating, but some species with lighter armor swam in the high seas. Some species, such as Dunkleosteus, were very large — over 13 feet (4 m) — and became aggressive predators.

Dunkleosteus was a powerful, frightening predator. Its huge skull measured over 25 inches (65 cm).

Bothriolepis lived on the seabed because of the weight of its armor.

that some predators wait for the salmon's arrival?

Many animals know that the salmon swimming upstream in mating season are adults with tasty flesh. The salmon are also less wary of their enemies during this time. Some animals make the most of this source of food.

Bears, for example, gather around rivers during the salmon mating season. They lie in wait in strategic positions near waterfalls the salmon must climb. With a quick thrust of their paws, they catch the passing fish.

THE LIFE OF THE SALMON

The salmon's growth

During reproduction, the female salmon lays approximately 450 to 800 eggs per pound (.5 kilogram) of its body weight. Each egg measures about .3 inches (7 millimeters) in diameter and is translucent. At hatching time, each fry is about .5 inches (13 mm) long. For the first few weeks, it survives off the yolk sac that hangs from its belly.

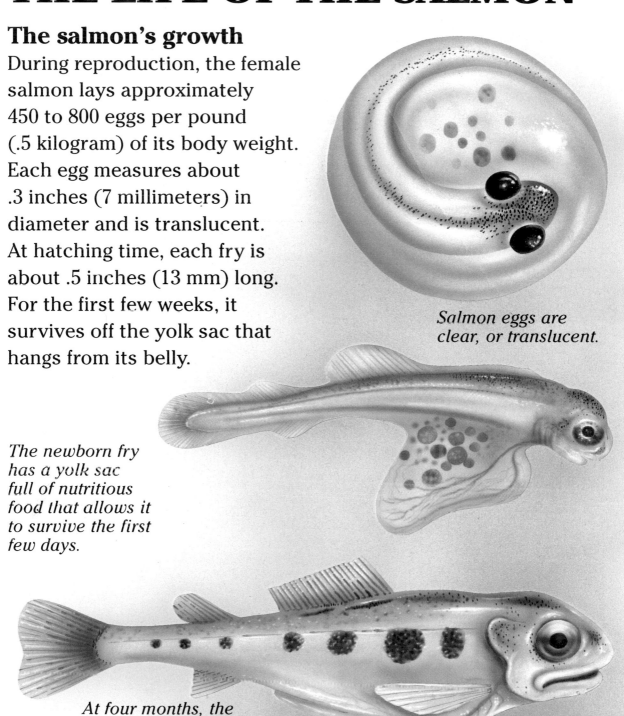

Salmon eggs are clear, or translucent.

The newborn fry has a yolk sac full of nutritious food that allows it to survive the first few days.

At four months, the fry measures about 1 inch (3 cm).

When salmon reach about 3 inches (7 cm) in length, dark spots appear on their bodies, and they are called "piebalds." They look this way for the first two years while continuing to grow, until they feel the urge to go to the sea where they develop into adults.

Salmon are aggressive predators that hunt their prey, usually fish and shellfish.

A two-year-old salmon, called a piebald because of its spots, can measure up to 8 inches (20 cm).

An adult salmon can weigh over 65 pounds (30 kg) and measure 5 feet (1.5 m).

that salmon have to adapt to changes in salinity?

Some fish — such as salmon, eels, and lamprey — spend part of their lives in fresh water, and another part in salt water. Some young salmon leave their river homes after one year; others wait two or three years. To survive the new conditions, their bodies must change before going from one environment to another. Some glands become more active, the salmon's endurance increases, and its senses become sharper.

APPENDIX TO

SECRETS OF THE ANIMAL WORLD

SALMON
Tireless Travelers

SALMON SECRETS

▼ Changes in the male salmon. Before migrating to the mating grounds, the male's lower jaw develops a hooklike "weapon." The salmon use this weapon in the violent combat between males over females during mating rituals.

▼ Differences between the sexes. Male and female salmon differ quite a bit in size. Females rarely weigh over 45 pounds (20 kg) or measure more than 3 feet (1 m) in length. Males, on the other hand, can weigh more than 75 pounds (35 kg) and measure over 5 feet (1.5 m) in length.

Going back home. Families of salmon, generation after generation, always return to the same stream to reproduce. For this reason, it is common for salmon from different rivers to follow different evolutionary patterns, even though the rivers are not geographically far from each other.

Salmon and the magnetic field. Some scientists believe that salmon, besides using their sense of smell during migration, are also able to find their bearings using Earth's magnetic field or the stars, just as birds do.

▼ Salmon farms. In some areas of the world, open waters are roped, or cordoned, off to breed salmon for commercial purposes.

Super Salmon. Some scientists have tried breeding salmon by choosing those that grow fastest and healthiest. After eighteen years, they have obtained bigger and heavier salmon that reach sexual maturity early — truly super salmon!

1. An adult salmon can measure:
   a) over 1.5 feet (.5 m).
   b) over 5 feet (1.5 m).
   c) over 8 feet (2.5 m).

2. Agnaths are:
   a) glands on the fins.
   b) fish without jaws.
   c) salmon eggs.

3. During migration, salmon usually travel:
   a) about 125-185 miles (200-300 km).
   b) about 6,200 miles (10,000 km).
   c) about 8,700 miles (14,000 km).

4. Salmon can jump:
   a) 3 feet (1 m) high and 6.5 feet (2 m) in length.
   b) 6.5 feet (2 m) high and 6.5 feet (2 m) in length.
   c) 6.5 feet (2 m) high and 13 feet (4 m) in length.

5. Salmon nests measure:
   a) about 3 feet (1 m) in length and 2-4 inches (5-10 cm) deep.
   b) about 1 foot (30 cm) long and 12-14 inches (30-35 cm) deep.
   c) about 2 feet (60 cm) in length and 3-6.5 feet (1-2 m) deep.

The answers to SALMON SECRETS questions are on page 32.

GLOSSARY

adapt: to make changes or adjustments in order to survive in a changing environment.

aggressive: bold; eager to confront or engage in combat.

ancestors: previous generations; predecessors.

aquatic: of or relating to water; living or growing in water.

armor: a protective covering.

breed (v): to mate a male and a female together for the purpose of producing young.

buoyancy: the ability to float in a body of water.

current: a flowing mass of air or water.

devour: to eat hungrily or greedily.

endurance: the ability to keep going in spite of many difficulties or obstacles; the ability to withstand hardship or pain.

environment: the surroundings in which plants, animals, and other organisms live.

evolve: to change or develop gradually from one form to another. Over time, all living things must evolve to survive in their changing environments, or they may become extinct.

exhaustion: the state of being extremely tired or worn out.

fertilize: to make ready for reproduction, growth, or development, usually by adding something that is not present.

fry: recently hatched fishes.

fusiform: shaped like a torpedo; having a shape that is tapered at both ends.

genus (*plural* genera): according to the biological classification system, the main subdivision of a family that includes one or more species. There are four genera of salmon: Salmo, Salvelinus, Oncorhynchus, and Coregonus.

gills: the breathing organs in all fish, also known as branchiae.

glands: organs in the body that make and release substances such as sweat, tears, and saliva.

glide: to move smoothly, quietly, and easily.

hydroelectric: generating electricity from water power.

instinct: a natural (as opposed to learned) ability or behavior.

magnetic field: the area or space around a magnet or magnetic body within which the magnetic force can be detected.

mate (v): to join together to produce young.

microscopic: too small to be seen with the human eye; capable of being seen only through a microscope.

migrate: to move from one place or climate to another, usually on a seasonal basis.

obstacle: something that blocks or stands in the way.

operculum: a lid or covering flap.

parallel: lying in the same horizontal plane but not touching at any point.

plankton: tiny plants and animals that drift in rivers, lakes, and oceans.

predators: animals that kill and eat other animals.

prey: animals that are hunted, captured, and killed for food by other animals.

primitive: of or relating to an early and usually simple stage of development.

propel: to move in a forward direction.

regulate: to control or direct in some way.

reproduce: to mate, create offspring, and bear young.

reserve: a supply or store of something that is set aside for later use.

salinity: the amount of salt in water or soil.

Salmonidae: in the biological classification system, the name for the salmon family; its members are elongated, soft-finned fish, such as salmon and trout.

scales: small, thin, platelike pieces that overlap to cover the bodies of fish and reptiles.

snout: protruding nose and jaw of an animal.

spawning grounds: areas where large numbers of fish lay their eggs.

species: animals or plants that are closely related and often similar in behavior and appearance. Members of the same species are able to breed together.

sturdy: strongly made or built.

tireless: able to keep working or moving for a long time without getting fatigued.

translucent: clear; allowing light to pass through so that objects on the inside or other side are visible.

yolk sac: a membranous bag containing egg yolk.

ACTIVITIES

◆ The salmon is not the only fish that migrates between fresh water and ocean to complete its life cycle. The common eel also travels between sea and river in order to spawn. Go to the library and do research about this fish. What ocean is part of the eel's life cycle? From which shores flow the rivers where eels can be found? How long does it take a newly hatched eel to grow until it is ready to spawn? Draw a map of both the salmon and eel migration paths and compare the distances. Which fish must swim the farthest before it can spawn?

◆ Fishing for salmon, tuna, herring, cod, and many other kinds of fish provides large amounts of nourishing food for humans and livestock. Find some books in your library about the fishing industries. What other countries depend on fishing to help feed their population? Recently, cod have become too depleted to be fished any longer. Do you think the amount of fish taken each year should be limited? How does pollution affect the stocks of fish in the sea? What can be done to overcome the harm being done to food fish?

MORE BOOKS TO READ

Amazing Fish. Mary Ling (Knopf)
The Atlantic Salmon. Bianca Lavies (Dutton)
Extremely Weird Fish. Sarah Lovett (John Muir)
Fearsome Fish. Steve Parker (Raintree Steck-Vaughn)
Fish. Mark Evans (Dorling Kindersley)
Fish. Colin S. Milkins (Thomson Learning)
Red Tag Comes Back. Frederick B. Phleger (HarperCollins)
The Salmon. Paula Z. Hogan (Raintree Steck-Vaughn)
Salmon Story. Brenda Z. Guiberson (Henry Holt & Co.)
What Is a Fish? Barbara R. Stratton (Franklin Watts)

VIDEOS

Life of the Sockeye Salmon. (Journal Films and Video)
Looking at Fishes. (Encyclopædia Britannica Educational Corporation)
Salmon on the Line. (Portland State University)
Salmon on the Run. Nova series. (Ambrose Video Publishing)
The Tragedy of the Red Salmon. Undersea World of Jacques Cousteau
  series. (Churchill Media)

PLACES TO VISIT

Seattle Aquarium
Pier 59
Waterfront Park
Seattle, WA 98101

New England Aquarium
Central Wharf
Boston, MA 02110

Australian Museum
6-8 College Street
Sydney, Australia 2000

Museum of Victoria
222 Exhibition Street
Melbourne, Victoria
Australia 3000

**Fisheries Museum of the
    Atlantic**
Bluenose Drive
Lunenburg, Nova Scotia
B0J 2C0

Pacific Undersea Gardens
490 Belleville Street
Victoria, British Columbia
V8V IW9

Otago Museum
419 Great King Street
Dunedin, New Zealand

INDEX

Answers to SALMON SECRETS questions:
1. **b**
2. **b**
3. **a**
4. **c**
5. **a**